Everyday Material Science Experiments

METALS

Robert C. Mebane
Thomas R. Rybolt

Illustrations by Anni Matsick

TWENTY-FIRST CENTURY BOOKS
A Division of Henry Holt and Company
New York

Twenty-First Century Books
A Division of Henry Holt and Company, Inc.
115 West 18th Street
New York, NY 10011

Henry Holt® and colophon are trademarks of
Henry Holt and Company, Inc.
Publishers since 1866

Published in Canada by Fitzhenry & Whiteside Ltd.
195 Allstate Parkway, Markham, Ontario L3R 4T8

Library of Congress Cataloging-in-Publication Data

Mebane, Robert C.
Metals / Robert C. Mebane and Thomas R. Rybolt;
illustrations by Anni Matsick.—1st ed.
p. cm. — (Everyday material science experiments)
Includes bibliographical references and index.
1. Metals—Experiments—Juvenile literature. [1. Metals—Experiments.
2. Experiments.] I. Rybolt, Thomas R. II. Matsick, Anni, ill. III. Title.
IV. Series: Mebane, Robert C. Everyday material science experiments.
TA459.M282 1995
669—dc20 94–43110
CIP
AC

ISBN 0–8050–2842–0
First Edition 1995

Designed by Kelly Soong

Printed in Mexico
All first editions are printed on acid-free paper ∞.
10 9 8 7 6 5 4 3 2 1

For Charliann and Chelsea Heather, with love —R.M.

For my nieces, Lisa Rybolt and Sara Rybolt —T.R.

ACKNOWLEDGMENT

We wish to thank Professor Mickey Sarquis of Miami University, Middletown, Ohio, for reading and making helpful comments on the manuscript.

CONTENTS

INTRODUCTION

The world around you is filled with ***Air and Other Gases, Water and Other Liquids, Salts and Solids, Metals,*** and ***Plastics and Polymers.*** Some of these materials are part of our natural environment, and some are part of our created, industrial environment. The materials that we depend on for life and the materials that are part of our daily living all have distinct properties. These properties can be best understood through careful examination and experimentation.

Have you ever wondered why some metals are shiny, how a magnet works, how a fuse protects electrical circuits, or why a metal spoon warms quickly in a hot liquid? In this book you will discover answers to these and many other fascinating questions about ***Metals.*** In the process you will learn about metals as materials—what they are made of, how they behave, and why they are important.

Each experiment is designed to stand alone. That is, it's not necessary to start with the first experiment and proceed to the second, then the third, and so on. Feel free to skip around—that's part of the fun of discovery. As you do the experiments, think about the results and what they mean to you. Also, think about how the results apply to the world around you.

At the beginning of each experiment, you will find one or more icons identifying the important physical science concept dealt with in the experiment. For example, if the icon ❋ appears at the top of the page, it means that matter, one of the basic concepts of science, will be explored. On page 61, you will find a listing of all the icons—matter, energy, light, heat, sound, electricity, and magnetism—and the experiments to which they relate.

As you carry out the experiments in this book, be sure to follow carefully any special safety instructions that are given. **For some experiments, a ❗ means that you should have an adult work with you.** For all your experiments, you need to make sure that an adult knows what you are doing. Remember to clean up after your experiment is completed.

1

THE TRANSFER OF HEAT THROUGH SOLIDS

MATERIALS NEEDED

- Three water glasses (the glasses need to be shorter than the spoons)
- Ice
- Water
- Three plastic spoons
- Three stainless-steel spoons
- Watch or clock

In this experiment you will explore how metals conduct, or carry, heat from one place to another.

Fill the first glass with ice cubes and add enough water to bring the level of water to the top of the glass. Leave the second glass empty. Run hot water from a faucet into a sink for several minutes until the water is quite hot, then fill the third glass with hot water. Place one plastic spoon and one stainless-steel spoon in each of the three glasses, as shown in Figure A.

After 10 minutes, feel the end of each spoon sticking out of the glasses. Which spoon is the hottest? Which spoon is the coldest? Is there a difference between the plastic and metal spoons?

You should find that the metal spoon in the cold ice water became cool, but the plastic spoon did not. You should find that the metal spoon in the hot water got warm, while the plastic spoon did not.

Heat moves through a solid by a means called *conduction*. In

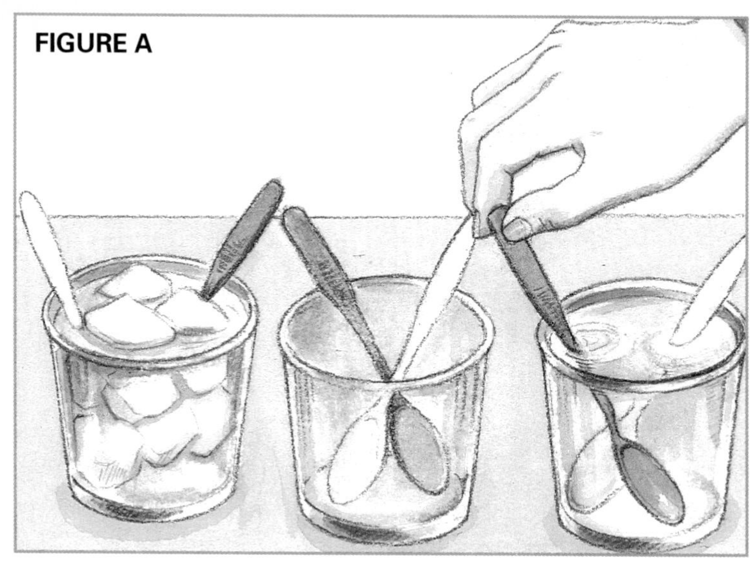
FIGURE A

conduction, heat is transferred through a solid because the atoms in the solid are always moving back and forth. Although the atoms stay in fixed positions, they still can bump and jostle atoms near them. In the nineteenth century, scientists realized that heat is the energy of motion of atoms and molecules. Scientists also discovered that heat always goes from a region of higher temperature to a region of lower temperature (from hot to cold), as shown in Figure B.

Imagine a crowd of people packed together but standing fairly still. If people at one end of the crowd began pushing and shoving people near them, then those people who got pushed

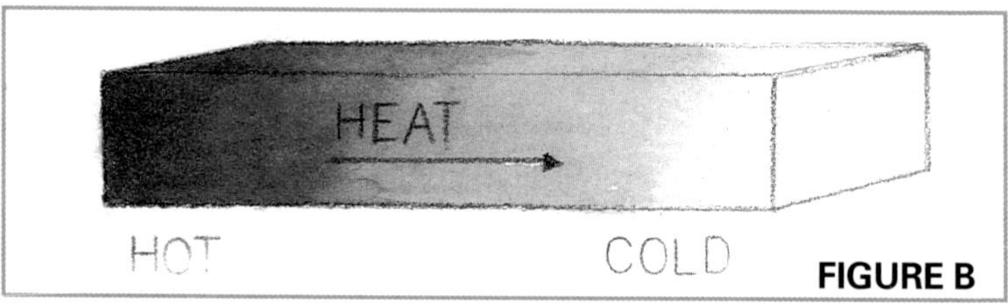

FIGURE B

would bump into people near them. You could imagine that the pushing and shoving would not stop but would spread throughout the entire crowd of people. In a similar way, the greater energy of motion associated with hot atoms tends to spread to cooler atoms nearby. The atoms bump and jostle other atoms nearby and the heat spreads throughout the solid.

As the temperature of a metal is raised, the metal atoms move about more and more rapidly. For the metal spoon placed in hot water, the heat travels from the water into the spoon and then up the spoon toward the cooler end in the air. For the spoon placed in the cold ice water, the heat travels out of the spoon into the colder water. As the end of the spoon in the water becomes cooler, the heat from the hotter end travels down the spoon toward the cooler end in the water. Because heat flows out of the spoon, the spoon feels cold when you touch it.

If there is a temperature difference across a metal so that one end is hot and the other end is cold, what will happen? We always find that the hot end becomes cooler and the cold end becomes warmer. This flow of heat will continue until the two ends are exactly the same temperature. When there is no longer any difference in temperature, then there will be no more flow of heat energy.

Metals are good conductors of heat. Heat travels fairly rapidly through a metal but only slowly through an insulator material like plastic. Wood and plastic are such poor conductors of heat that they are called *insulators*. The atoms in a plastic spoon are locked more rigidly into fixed positions because they are part of long polymer molecules. Heat cannot travel as well through the plastic spoon as it can through the metal spoon because the atoms cannot jostle and bump one another as they can in a metal. Why does a metal cooking pan often have a plastic or wooden handle?

EXPANDING A METAL WITH HEAT

MATERIALS NEEDED

- Bare copper wire, 40 in. (about 100 cm) long (available in hardware and electronic supply stores)
- Two wooden chairs
- Wrench
- Index card
- Metal pan
- Matches
- Candle

Alert! Adult supervision needed.

Have you ever wondered why mercury metal rises in a thermometer as the temperature increases? In this experiment you will explore how heat and increasing temperature can change the size of a metal.

Bend about 5 in. (13 cm) of wire around a back post of one wooden chair and twist the wire together so that it is firmly attached to the chair. Slip the free end of the wire through a wrench so that the wrench hangs from the wire. Take the free end of the wire and bend about 5 in. (13 cm) of it around a back post of the other wooden chair. Once again, twist this wire to firmly attach it to the second chair.

Move the chairs so the wrench hangs from the middle of the wire, halfway between the two chairs. Place an index card on the floor underneath the wrench. Now carefully adjust the distance between the chairs to lower the wrench until it is just barely above the index card. You should still be able to slide the card freely along the floor without moving the wrench. For the rest of the experiment, be careful not to bump or move either of the chairs.

Set the metal pan on the floor between the wrench and one of the chairs. Light a candle and hold it above the metal pan, as shown in Figure A. The metal pan protects the floor from wax that may drip off the candle. Hold the candle so the flame is directly on the wire and move the candle slightly so that a small portion of the wire becomes extremely hot.

As the wire is being heated, carefully observe the position of the wrench above the index card. Does the height of the wrench change? After several minutes of heating the wire, check and see if the wrench is touching the index card on the floor. Slide the index card back and forth slightly and see if the wrench moves. Can you explain what has happened to the wire and the wrench? Now blow out the candle and watch the wrench. What happens?

The wrench should be touching the card after the candle flame heats the wire. When you slide the card the wrench moves, so you know that the wrench is closer to the floor than it was before the wire was heated. Since the chairs were not moved, then the wire must have been changed by the heat. If the wrench is lower, then the wire must have gotten longer. When the candle flame is blown out, the wire cools, and the wrench should move back to its original, higher position.

Heating a metal causes it to expand. The small portion of wire that was heated not only got hotter, but also got longer, or expanded. Cooling a metal causes it to contract, or get smaller.

Heat is the energy of the random motion of atoms and molecules, and when a solid is heated, its atoms move more rapidly. Although the atoms are in fixed positions like bricks in a wall, they still vibrate back and forth and jostle one another. In a packed crowd of people, one person may not be able to move past another but can still be bumped and made to move against people nearby. If each person in a crowd is moving back and forth, everyone will not be able to pack together as closely as if they were all standing extremely still. The same is true for atoms in a solid

metal. As a wire is heated, the atoms move about more. Since each atom takes up more room, the metal expands.

In a mercury thermometer, we can see that these metal atoms take up more room when they become hotter. As the temperature of a thermometer increases, the mercury atoms jostle one another more rapidly and take up more space, causing the liquid mercury to expand higher in the narrow tube that holds it. The temperature is indicated by the level of the mercury. Mercury is one of a few metals that is liquid at room temperature.

Can you think of other examples of solids expanding or contracting with temperature changes? Can you explain why the steel beams used in constructing large buildings and bridges are placed so there are expansion joints or spaces between the beams?

3

BREAKING METAL

MATERIALS NEEDED

- A large, shiny, metal paper clip
- A small bowl
- Marbles

Have you ever had a piece of metal on a bicycle, cart, or other object crack and eventually break? How does metal break? To learn more, try this experiment.

Partially straighten a large, shiny, metal paper clip. Touch the paper clip to your lower lip to feel its temperature. Hold the straightened portion of the paper clip with the thumb and forefinger of your right hand next to the thumb and forefinger of your left hand, as shown in Figure A. Your hands should be close together. Bend the paper clip back and forth five to six times and then immediately touch the paper clip to your lower lip. How does the paper clip feel? Look closely at the spot on the paper clip that was bent. Describe how it looks. You may notice that this spot is no longer shiny, but in fact has turned dull. You may even see tiny cracks in the metal.

Continue to bend the paper clip back and forth with both hands until it breaks. You should feel that the paper clip becomes easier to bend as you approach its breaking point. Examine and describe the break. Does the break appear jagged and dull?

The atoms in metals pack closely together in a regular, repeating pattern called a *metal crystal*. To help you imagine what

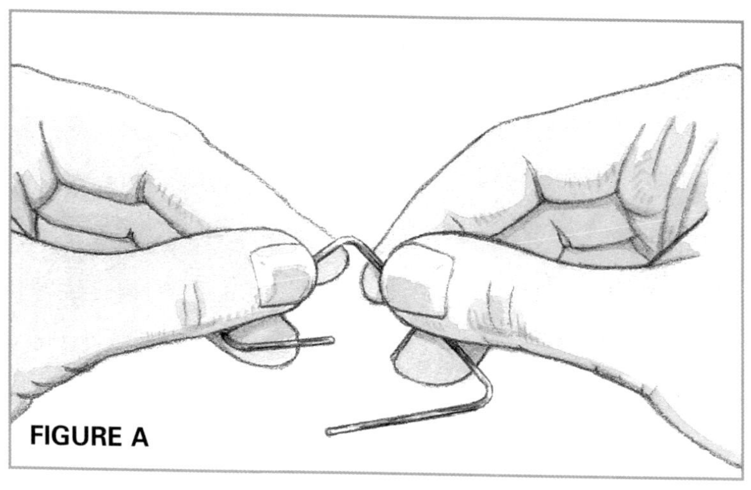
FIGURE A

a metal crystal looks like, fill a small bowl nearly full with marbles. You will notice that the marbles pack closely together and that each marble touches many other ones. In many metals, each atom in a metal crystal touches 12 other atoms. Electrons around the atoms act like a glue to hold the atoms close to one another in a crystal. These electrons are free to move around all the atoms in a metal crystal.

When most metals are struck hard with a force, they change shape or form, rather than shatter. Metals change shape easily because the closely packed atoms in the metal crystals can slide over one another when they are subjected to a force or push. The free electrons help hold the moving atoms together. Metals that can be hammered or beaten into different shapes are called *malleable*. Metals that can be pulled or drawn into a wire are called *ductile*.

A repeated stress, such as bending a piece of metal back and forth, can disrupt the closely packed atoms in the metal crystal. The atoms in the metal crystal become less ordered and more random. Friction from the metal atoms moving over one another generates heat, which also disrupts the ordered packing of the atoms in the crystal. Tiny fractures may develop between atoms in the crystal. If the stress continues, the fractures may enlarge, and the metal breaks into pieces where the stress is applied. The tendency of a metal to break under the application of a repeated stress is called *metal fatigue*.

In this experiment you cause fatigue in the metal of the paper clip when you bend it back and forth. After bending the paper clip five or six times, you should have noticed that the portion of the paper clip being bent was warm. Do you know why? Also, the surface of the metal was no longer shiny, but dull. These are signs of metal fatigue.

The change from shiny to dull on the surface of the paper clip is due to tiny fractures that have developed in the metal. You may even be able to see tiny cracks in the metal that indicate that the fractures in the metal have enlarged.

Continued bending of the paper clip enlarges the fractures and cracks in the metal and the metal breaks into pieces. The jagged appearance of the break indicates that there were many fractures caused by the metal fatigue.

Metal objects that must support weight (like steel beams) or ones that move rapidly (like turbines in jet engines) are subject to metal fatigue. If metal fatigue goes undetected, then the metal object may break suddenly without warning. A number of airplane accidents have been linked to metal fatigue of certain components in the airplanes. Numerous techniques, from visual inspections with a special microscope to the use of X rays, have been developed to detect metal fatigue. These techniques are routinely used during the inspection of metal components that are subjected to repeated stress.

MELTING METAL

MATERIALS NEEDED

- Solder, lead-free
- Oven
- Aluminum foil, heavy-duty
- Wire cutter or pliers
- Clock or watch
- Oven mitt
- Hot pad
- Long nail

Alert! Adult supervision needed.

For this experiment you will need to use plumbers solder that contains only tin and silver. This type of solder is often called silver solder and can be found in most hardware stores. Do not use solder that contains lead because lead can be toxic if ingested or inhaled. Also, do not use silver solder that contains flux and is used to make electrical connections, as flux can produce fumes when heated.

Turn on the oven and set its temperature to 500°F (260°C). While the oven is heating, take a piece of heavy-duty aluminum foil about 12 in. (30 cm) long and fold it to form a small boat. Cut a piece of silver solder about 3 in. (7.5 cm) in length with a wire cutter or pliers. Place the solder in the aluminum boat. You may need to bend the length of solder so that it completely rests on the bottom of your aluminum boat.

Place the aluminum boat containing the solder in the hot oven and close the oven door. After 5 minutes, check to see if the solder has melted. The solder will form a puddle when it has melted. If it has not melted, leave it in the hot oven an additional 5 minutes or until it has melted. When it has melted, remove the aluminum boat from the oven with an oven mitt and place it on a hot pad. Make sure to turn off the oven. Use a long nail to probe the molten solder. Be careful not to burn yourself. How long does it take for the molten solder to solidify?

Except for mercury, all metals are a solid at room temperature (room temperature is considered to be around 68°F [20°C]). Metals melt when heated to their melting point temperature, which is the temperature a solid changes to a liquid. The melting points of metals vary considerably, but they are usually high. Approximately 76 percent of all the pure metals have a melting point above 932°F (500°C). Tungsten, which is used for filaments in lightbulbs, has the highest melting point of all metals at 6170°F (3410°C). In contrast, mercury, which is used in some thermometers, is a liquid at room temperature and has a melting point of -37°F (-39°C). The melting points of some common metals, from highest to lowest, are:

iron	2798°F (1536°C)	zinc	787°F (419°C)
copper	1981°F (1083°C)	lead	621°F (327°C)
gold	1945°F (1063°C)	cadmium	610°F (321°C)
silver	1761°F (960°C)	bismuth	520°F (271°C)
aluminum	1220°F (660°C)	tin	449°F (232°C)

It is not possible to use a pure metal in this experiment because most of the readily available pure metals have melting points higher than the highest temperature of a kitchen oven, which is around 500°F (260°C). Instead, you use solder, which is an alloy. An *alloy* is a mixture of metals, or a mixture of a metal or metals with nonmetals. Two common alloys are bronze, a mixture of copper and tin, and brass, a combination of copper and zinc. A nickel coin is an alloy of copper and nickel.

There are several different kinds of solder. The kind used in this experiment, silver solder, is a mixture of tin and silver.

Since the melting point of this solder is around 450°F (232°C), it is easily melted in an oven.

You should notice that the solder collects in a puddle and moves freely when it melts. You may also notice some dark, grayish material on the shiny surface of the molten solder. This grayish material is probably impurities in the solder that have floated to the surface. When the temperature of the molten solder falls below its melting point, it becomes a solid again.

Generally, alloys have melting points lower than the melting points of the metals used to make the alloy. A unique example is Wood's metal, which melts at 158°F (70°C) and is an alloy of bismuth, lead, tin, and cadmium. Because of its low melting point, Wood's metal is used to make electrical fuses and automatic sprinkler heads for fire protection. Can you think of any other uses for a metal or alloy with a low melting point?

5

BURNING METAL

MATERIALS NEEDED

- Gloves
- Safety glasses or goggles
- Water
- Fine steel wool
- Pliers
- Match or lighter
- Coarse steel wool

Alert! Adult supervision needed. Gloves and eye protection, such as safety glasses or goggles, should be worn.

You have probably seen many things burn—like paper, wood, charcoal, and gas. Have you ever seen a piece of metal burn? Do you think metal can burn like paper? To find out, try this experiment.

Close the drain to a sink. Add water until the bottom of the sink is just covered. Pull a piece of steel wool about the size of a quarter from a pad of fine steel wool. The small piece of steel wool should be loose and not wadded into a ball.

Grasp the small piece of steel wool with a pair of pliers, as shown in Figure A. While holding the steel wool in the sink about 2 in. (5 cm) above the water, touch the steel wool to the flame of a lit match or lighter. Does the fine steel wool burn? Before you discard the burned steel wool in the trash, place it underwater for 10 seconds.

Repeat this experiment using a small piece of coarse steel wool. Does the coarse steel wool burn as easily as the fine steel

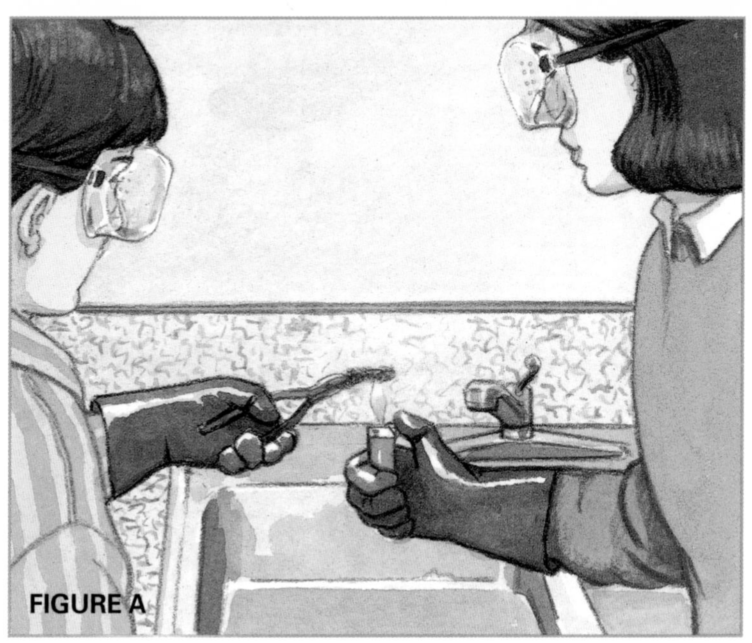
FIGURE A

wool? Make sure to completely immerse the piece of steel wool in water before you discard it in the trash.

When the flame is touched to the piece of fine steel wool, you should observe that the steel wool burns rather quickly. As the steel wool burns, heat and light are generated, just as they are generated in the burning of familiar substances such as wood, paper, and coal. The formation of heat and light indicates that energy is released in the burning process.

Usually when we think about burning a substance, we think about burning fuels such as wood, coal, natural gas, and oil. But metals can also be made to burn.

When fuels burn, oxygen from the air combines with the carbon and hydrogen in the fuel to form new chemical substances. If enough oxygen is present, and the burning is complete, then the new chemical substances made during burning are mostly carbon dioxide and water.

The burning of the steel wool is basically the same as the

burning of fuels, except that oxygen from the air combines with the iron in the steel wool (steel wool is mostly iron metal) to change the iron into iron oxide. Just as when fuels burn, energy, in the form of heat and light, is released when the iron burns.

You should notice that the fine steel wool burns more easily than the coarse steel wool. This is because the fine steel wool has a lower kindling temperature. The *kindling temperature* is the temperature at which burning generates enough heat to keep the burning process going without the further addition of heat.

Iron, and most metals, have high kindling temperatures, so objects made out of metal, such as iron nails, do not burn. On the other hand, if the iron is in the form of a fine wire or fine powder, then the kindling temperature of the iron becomes low enough so that it burns readily. The fine strands of iron or powdered iron have a greater surface area, and thus, more iron metal is exposed to oxygen in the air.

Large pieces of iron do react with oxygen to form rust, but the process, which is a type of corrosion, is slow. Both corrosion and the burning of steel wool are called *oxidation* because oxygen is involved in both processes.

Before the invention of the electronic flash, powdered magnesium, and later fine magnesium wire encased in a glass bulb, was burned to produce a flash of light for making photographic pictures. Finely powdered iron, aluminum, and magnesium are used in fireworks and in signaling flares to make brilliant white flames and sparks.

LIGHT FROM A METAL

MATERIALS NEEDED

- Chair
- Table
- Magicube (nonbattery flashcube available where film is sold)
- Book
- Pencil

Alert! Adult supervision needed.

Have you ever seen a flash from a camera that uses disposable flashbulbs? In this experiment, you will explore what happens to the metal in this type of flashbulb.

Sit in a chair in front of a table. Set a Magicube flashcube upside down on the table and set a book upright on the table between you and the flashcube. The book will shield your eyes from the direct light of the flash. Hold the Magicube flat on the table with one hand. Pick up a pencil with your other hand.

There are four openings into the base of the Magicube. There is a small wire across the center of each opening, as shown in Figure A. Place the point of a pencil against one of these wires, as shown in Figure B. Lean back so you cannot see the flashcube. If the pencil is in your right hand, you will pull the point of the pencil toward you. If the pencil is in your left hand, you will push the point of the pencil away from you. **Do not look directly at the flash.** Now push or pull on the pencil and you will feel the wire

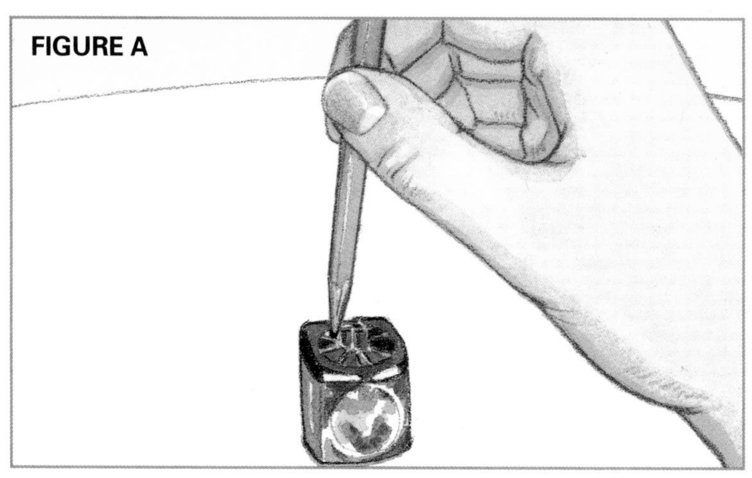
FIGURE A

FIGURE B

move slightly. Quickly lift the pencil and the wire will snap back against the base of one of the four flashbulbs. What happens?

When the wire snaps against the base of the bulb, a flash of light should be given off, and the bulb should become warm.

Look carefully at the bulb that has flashed and compare it to the other bulbs that have not flashed. In the flashed bulb, do you see small globs of solid on the inside walls of the glass bulb?

In the unflashed bulbs, there is a thin, shiny wire of magnesium and the bulb is filled with oxygen gas. When a pulse of electricity enters the bulb, it begins a chemical reaction between the magnesium metal and the oxygen. In this reaction, the magnesium combines with oxygen to form magnesium oxide. Energy, in the form of light and heat, is also released.

Electrical energy to ignite the magnesium comes from the use of a piezoelectric material. A crystal solid that is piezoelectric can convert mechanical energy to electricity or convert electrical energy to mechanical movement in the crystal. If a piezoelectric crystal, such as barium titanate, is subject to some mechanical stress—being struck, for example—an electric charge is produced.

The disposable (one-time use) flashbulb was invented in 1929 and used electric current from a battery to ignite the wire in the bulb. Magicubes are a type of disposable bulb that does not require the use of a battery. However, today most cameras use a reusable electronic flash.

Some metals, like gold, do not react with oxygen in the air. Other metals, like copper, react slowly over a period of years. Some metals, like magnesium, if ignited by a spark or flame, can react very rapidly and give off heat and light.

In this experiment you have seen a rapid combination of oxygen with a metal. This process, which is called oxidation, can also occur extremely slowly. Look at a new, shiny penny and an older, dull penny. The new penny is covered with copper metal, which reflects light and is shiny. What do you think has happened to the older penny to turn it to a dull color that does not reflect light?

MAKING A FUSE

MATERIALS NEEDED

- 6-volt flashlight lantern with battery
- Three wires with alligator clips on each end
- Coarse steel wool
- Glass jar with a wide mouth

Alert! Adult supervision needed.

In this experiment you will learn how a metal can protect electrical devices and make electricity safer to use. You will do this by making a fuse from a strand of coarse steel wool and testing it in an electrical circuit.

Remove the lamp housing and battery from a 6-volt flashlight lantern. Connect one end of a wire to the positive terminal of the battery. Connect one end of the second wire to the negative terminal of the battery. Next, determine how to connect the free ends of the wires coming from the battery to the lamp housing so that the bulb in the lamp housing lights up. There should be two metal contacts on the lamp housing for making a connection. Each lamp housing may be somewhat different, so you may have to experiment to make the proper connection. When you have made the proper connection and the bulb lights up, you have completed an electrical circuit.

Remove a strand of steel wool about 1 in. (2.5 cm) long from a pad of coarse steel wool. Attach one end of the third wire to one end of the strand of steel wool. Next, remove one of the alligator clips from the lamp housing and attach this clip to the strand of steel wool about 0.4 in. (1 cm) away from the alligator clip already attached to the strand.

Place your fuse with wires attached inside the jar. **Do not have any paper or other flammable material around the fuse.** Now take the free alligator clip and attach it to the lamp housing to complete the circuit, as shown in Figure A. You should observe that the bulb lights up and stays lit as long as the wires remain attached.

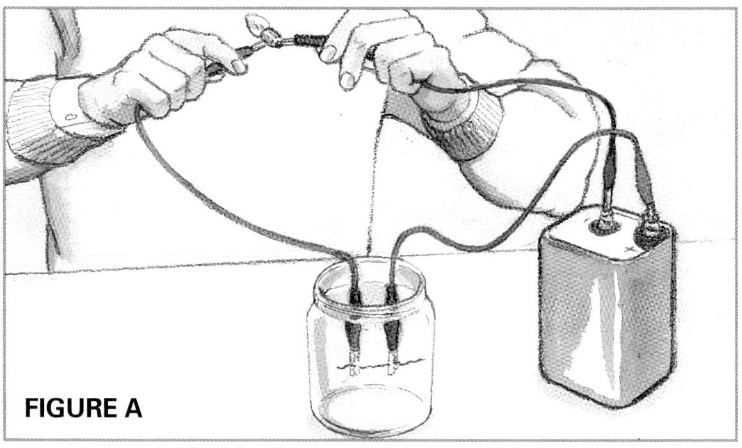

FIGURE A

To test your fuse you are going to cause a short circuit in your electrical circuit, as shown in Figure B. Remove the two alligator clips from the lamp housing and hold them in your hands. While observing the fuse, touch the two alligator clips together. What happens to the fuse?

You should observe that the fuse remains intact when your completed circuit includes the bulb, but quickly melts in two, or "blows," when the fuse is attached directly to the battery.

When a circuit is completed, electrons (electricity) flow from the electrical source, such as a battery, through the circuit and back to the electrical source. The amount of electrons that flow through a circuit is called the *current*, and the "pull," or force, on

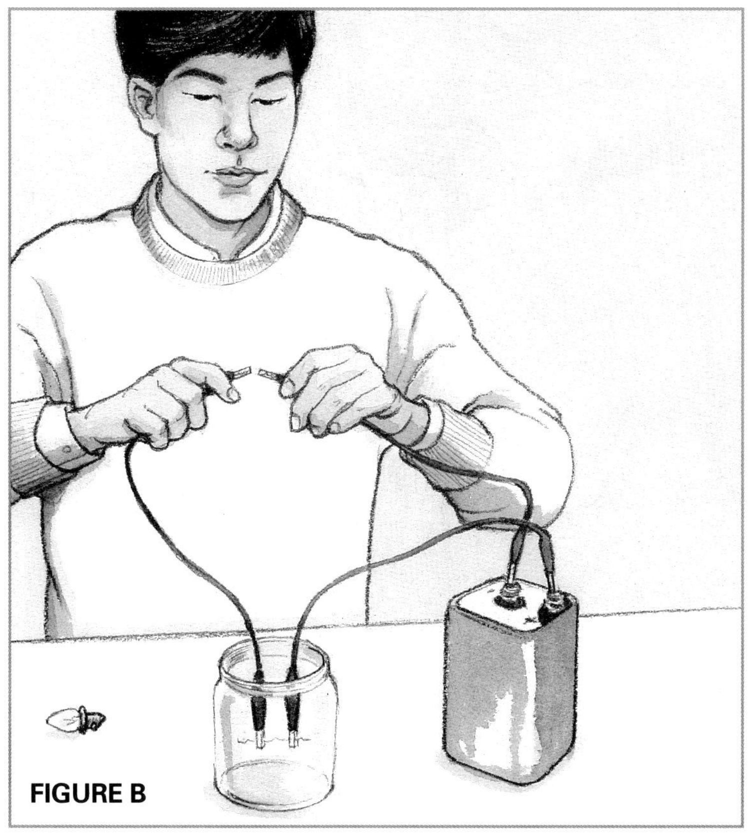
FIGURE B

the electrons to flow from the negative terminal to the positive terminal of the battery is called the *voltage*. In this experiment a battery with a voltage of 6 volts is used so the force on the electrons in your experiment is 6 volts.

In normal electrical circuits there is a natural tendency for the circuit to oppose or resist the flow of electrons through it. This is called the *resistance of the circuit*. The resistance of a circuit determines how much current can flow through the circuit. More current flows through a circuit with a low resistance than through a circuit with a high resistance. When electricity flows through a circuit that has a high resistance, some of the electrical energy is converted into other forms of energy such as heat, light, and sound.

The wire filament in the lamp bulb has a high resistance. This makes the circuit shown in Figure A have a high resistance. When the circuit in Figure A is completed, the resistance of the wire filament changes some of the electrical energy flowing through the filament into light and heat.

The circuit shown in Figure B is a short circuit because the resistance of the circuit is low. Both the wire and the fuse in the circuit have a low resistance. Since this circuit has a low resistance, the electricity travels a shorter path from the negative terminal to the positive terminal of the battery. This is why the circuit is called a *short circuit*.

Since the resistance of your short circuit is small, the current flow through the circuit will be large. As a result, the wire and the fuse of the short circuit will get hot. In fact, so much current flows through the short circuit that enough heat is produced in the circuit to actually melt the strand of steel wool used as a fuse. The fuse does not "blow" in the completed circuit shown in Figure A because the resistance of the lamp bulb does not allow enough current to flow through the strand of steel wool to make it hot enough to melt.

In 1880, Thomas Edison received a patent for inventing the first fuse to protect against overloads and short circuits. Modern fuses consist of a short piece of metal or metal wire enclosed in a protective covering. The protective covering is usually made of glass so you can tell if the fuse is good. The covering prevents hot, molten metal from coming in contact with something flammable when the fuse blows. The metal in a fuse is designed to melt when the current flowing through it reaches a certain value.

Circuit breakers are mechanical devices that are also used to protect electrical circuits from current overloads. Unlike a fuse, a circuit breaker can be reset after it has been "tripped." Nearly all homes built today are protected with circuit breakers. Why do you think it is important to have circuit breakers or fuses in home circuits?

8

METAL CORROSION

MATERIALS NEEDED

- Empty steel food can
- Magnet
- Iron nail
- Water
- Plastic bucket
- Stainless-steel screw

Each year, tens of billions of dollars are spent in the United States to repair and replace metal materials damaged by corrosion. Billions more are spent each year to protect metal products and materials from corrosion. Corrosion is a natural process, and although it cannot be stopped, it can be controlled. In the following experiment you will learn more about metal corrosion and how it is controlled.

For this experiment you will need a food can made of steel. Most food cans are made of steel or aluminum. You can use a magnet to test if a food can is made of steel or aluminum. Steel cans contain iron, which a magnet will attract. Aluminum is not attracted to a magnet. If a magnet sticks to the food can, it is made of steel.

Remove the label and clean and rinse your empty steel food can. **Be careful as you clean the can because the rim of the opened end may be sharp.** Take the nail and carefully scratch the can in several places. You can scratch a design or your initials on the can if you like.

Add water to a plastic bucket until the bottom of the bucket is just covered with a thin layer of water. Place the can, iron nail, and stainless-steel screw in the plastic bucket, as shown in Figure A. The metal items should not be completely covered with water. Put the bucket outside where it will not be disturbed. Observe the items in the bucket each day for a week. If all the water evaporates from the bucket before the week is up, add more water, enough to just cover the bottom of the bucket. What differences do you observe among the screw, nail, and can?

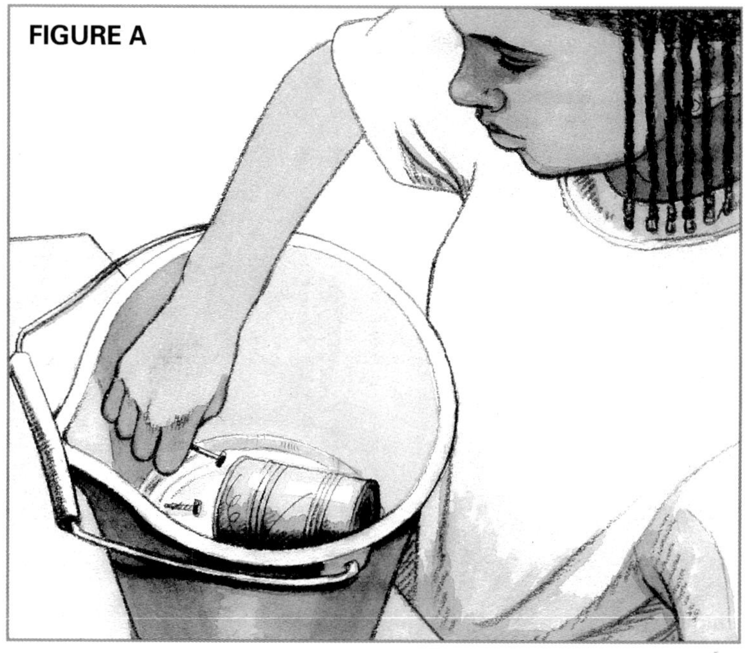
FIGURE A

After a couple of days you should notice that rust has formed on the iron nail and on the can where it was scratched. However, there should be no rust on the stainless-steel screw. As the days pass, more rust should form on both the food can and nail, but none on the stainless-steel screw.

The food can, nail, and stainless-steel screw all contain iron.

Iron is used far more than any other metal for making metal materials. Iron ore is abundant and is more easily converted into its pure form than other metals, such as aluminum. Aluminum is the most abundant metal in the earth's crust, but it requires great amounts of energy to convert its principal ore, bauxite, into pure aluminum.

Iron, like many metals, undergoes corrosion when exposed to air and water. The corrosion of iron involves a series of chemical reactions between oxygen in the air, water, and the iron metal. These reactions convert the iron into a chemical substance called *hydrated iron oxide,* the loose, flaky reddish brown substance we call iron rust. Water must be present for the reaction between oxygen and iron to occur. Iron that is perfectly dry does not corrode. This is why cars in the deserts of the Southwest last much longer than cars in wet areas of the country. Cars driven on roads where salt is used to melt snow and ice can rust extremely fast because salt accelerates the rusting process.

If left unchecked, corrosion can completely eat away and destroy items containing iron. Many methods have been used to prevent or retard the corrosion of iron. Two of these methods are explored in this experiment. Let's first consider the food can.

The steel used to make food cans is coated, or plated, with a thin layer of tin. This is why food cans are sometimes referred to as tin cans. The tin coating on a steel can is extremely thin, averaging about 0.00004 in. (0.001 mm). This is much thinner than the average diameter of a human hair, which is around 0.0012 in. (0.03 mm).

The thin coating of tin protects the steel underneath it from corrosion by keeping oxygen and water away from the steel. The tin on the surface of the coating reacts with oxygen in the air to form a hard, durable surface film of tin oxide. This layer of tin oxide serves as a protective barrier by preventing further contact between oxygen and the tin or steel in the can.

If the tin coating on a can becomes scratched and the scratch extends into the steel, then the steel will start to corrode when the can is exposed to air and water. This is why you should notice rust where you scratched your empty food can with a nail. If you leave your can outside long enough (months to years), it will eventually rust completely through.

Other metals, in addition to tin, are also used to coat steel to protect it from corrosion. Chrome bumpers on cars are actually mostly steel that is covered with a thin coating of chromium. *Galvanizing* is the process of applying a thin coat of zinc to the surface of an iron object to protect it from corrosion. The zinc protects the galvanized object by reacting with carbon dioxide in the air to form a layer of zinc carbonate over the entire surface. This protective layer of zinc carbonate keeps oxygen away from the underlying iron metal. Objects that often are galvanized include roofing nails, buckets, and wires.

Iron and steel also can be protected from corrosion by coating them with paint, lacquer, grease, or asphalt. The advantage to using these coatings is they can be easily applied over and over again. Bathtubs and sinks made of iron are protected from corrosion by a coating of ceramic. Ceramic enamel is also used to protect the steel in most refrigerators, stoves, and other large household appliances.

While the nail and the scratched food can rusted in this experiment, the stainless-steel screw probably did not. Stainless steel contains iron, chromium, nickel, and carbon. Stainless steel has a high resistance to rust and corrosion because the chromium and nickel in the steel react with oxygen in the air to form a protective coating on the surface of the stainless steel. Stainless steel is commonly used to make cooking utensils, plumbing fixtures, knives, instruments, and a variety of manufacturing machinery.

Several metals are extremely resistant to corrosion. These include copper, gold, silver, and platinum and are often referred to as *noble* or *precious metals*. Noble metals can be found in nature in a free or native state, which means the metals are not combined with other chemical elements. Copper, gold, and silver are also known as the *coinage metals* because of their use in the making of coins and durable ornamental objects.

Copper and silver will tarnish. Copper tarnishes by slowly reacting with carbon dioxide in the air to form the chemical substance *copper carbonate*. The bright green color often seen on copper roofs and statues is due to a layer of copper carbonate on the copper surface. Silver tarnishes when it reacts with sulfur compounds in the air.

MAKING A DIME LOOK LIKE A PENNY

MATERIALS NEEDED

- Uncoated, thick copper wire, 60 in. (152 cm) long (available at hardware or electronic supply stores)
- Salt shaker
- Small jar (baby-food size)
- 6-volt lantern battery
- Tablespoon
- Lemon juice
- Measuring cup
- Vinegar
- Insulated wire, 10 in. (25 cm) long (wire with clips on the ends is easiest to use)
- Dime
- Watch or clock
- Plastic clip (kind used to seal large potato chip bags)

In the Middle Ages, alchemists tried to transmute (change) inexpensive metals, such as lead, into more costly metals, such as gold. Although the alchemists were never able to transmute one metal into another, it may be possible to change the appearance of a metal. In this activity you will try to coat a dime with copper to make the dime look like a penny.

Use a 60-in. (152-cm) piece of bare copper wire and wrap it around a salt shaker or other small cylinder a dozen times, as shown in Figure A. This wrapping will make a coil of wire. Push the coiled part of the wire down into a small glass jar. The coiled wire should line the inside of the glass jar. Attach the free end of this wire to the positive terminal of a 6-volt lantern battery.

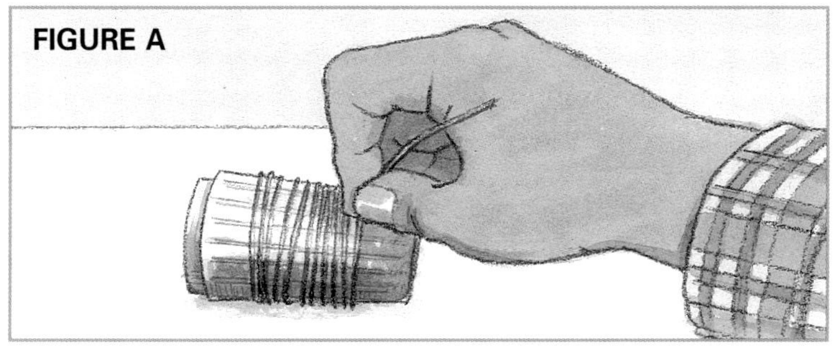
FIGURE A

Add 4 tablespoons (60 ml) of lemon juice to 1 cup (0.24 l) of vinegar and stir. Pour enough of this mixture to fill the small glass jar. Attach an insulated wire (wire with clips already attached works best) to the top of a dime. Attach the other end of this wire to the negative terminal of the battery. Place about half the dime in the liquid. The dime will need to stay in this position for about 50 minutes. You can use a plastic clip, such as the type used to seal bags, to hold the dime in place, as shown in Figure B. The dime should not touch the copper wire.

What happens when the dime is first placed into the vinegar? Remove the dime from the vinegar occasionally and look at the surface of the dime. Do you see any change? You may notice

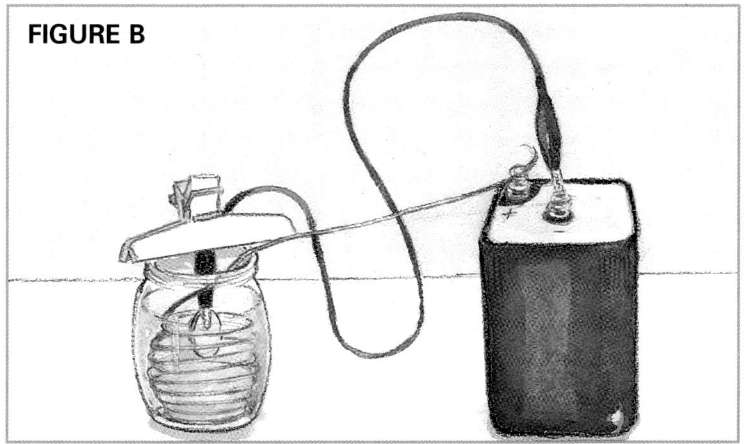

FIGURE B

that the vinegar and lemon juice mixture has changed to a blue color. After 50 minutes disconnect the wires from the battery, remove the dime from the vinegar solution, discard the vinegar solution in a sink, and thoroughly wash the glass jar.

The part of the dime that was immersed in the liquid should have a dark copperlike appearance. The part that remained above the liquid should be unchanged.

The blue color that gradually forms indicates that copper is present in the solution. Copper atoms come from the coil of copper wire. A copper atom in the wire gives up 2 electrons, and the newly formed positive (+2) copper atom, called an *ion*, goes into the vinegar solution. As copper atoms give up electrons, the electrons flow through the wire toward the positive terminal of the battery. At the same time, the electrons flowing from the negative terminal of the battery into the dime cause the dime to combine with positive copper atoms (ions) in the solution. This process, called *electroplating*, forms copper atoms on the surface of the dime. Vinegar and lemon juice are used because they contain acids that cause the liquid to have positive and negative particles (ions). The ions help carry the charge between the copper wire and dime and complete the circuit.

Metal items are often coated to protect them from corrosion (wearing away at the surface) or to change their appearance. This coating is often very thin. A metal coating may be only 0.001 in. (0.025 mm) thick. For example, trays may be plated with silver to make them look like solid silver.

In nickel-chromium electroplating, steel is plated with nickel and chromium to protect the steel against corrosion and to make the surface shiny. Nickel and chromium plating is used for automobile parts such as bumpers and handles. Galvanized metals are made by coating iron or steel with zinc. Can you name other applications where you might want to change a metal's appearance or properties?

MAKING AND TESTING A BATTERY

MATERIALS NEEDED

- Two steel nails
- Lemon
- Two shiny pennies
- Earphone (from a small radio or tape player)

Have you ever wondered how a battery produces electricity? In this activity you will make a simple battery and use an earphone to find out whether the battery can produce a flow of electrons in a wire.

Use a nail to make a slit in the lemon peel. Make the slit about as wide as a penny. Push the penny down into the slit so that about half the penny is inside the lemon. Now push the nail into the lemon about 0.3 in. (0.8 cm) away from the penny.

Put the listening part of an earphone in your ear. Take the jack or plug portion of the earphone and touch it across the penny and nail, as shown in Figure A. There will be a black or dark ring separating the metal at the end of the plug from the metal at the base of the plug. This ring should be placed between the nail and penny so that the end of the metal plug is touching the nail and the base of the metal plug is touching the penny. Do you hear a noise? Take the plug off the nail and penny and then return it. Again, do you hear the noise from the earphone?

You should hear a crackling sound coming from the earphone whenever the plug of the earphone is placed across the

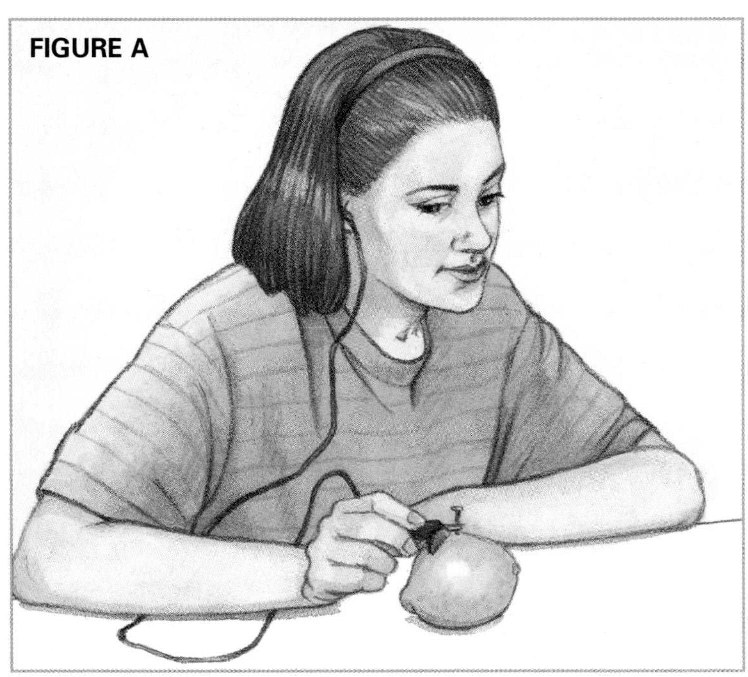

penny and nail to complete a circuit. Connecting the copper on the surface of the penny with the steel nail, which is mostly iron, makes a battery. Acid in the lemon contains charged molecules that can be used to complete the circuit between nail and penny.

In 1800 the Italian scientist Alessandro Volta connected different metals to make the first electric battery. He connected disks of copper and zinc or silver and zinc with cardboard soaked in salt water between each pair of disks. This pile of metal plates was used to produce a steady flow of electricity.

Some chemical reactions cause electrons to be given up in one place (oxidation) and taken in or added to a metal or other substance in another place (reduction). When these two types of chemical reactions are connected by a metal wire, then electrons can flow from the negative terminal, where oxidation occurs. The electrons are pushed through the wire toward the positive end of the battery, where reduction occurs, and then the electrons are pulled from the wire. The voltage a battery produces is a measure of this difference in the push and pull of electrons through a wire. An electronic device called a *voltmeter* can be used to measure the voltage of small batteries, including the one you made with steel and a copper-coated penny.

Your "lemon battery" does not produce enough current or flow of electrons to light a lightbulb or turn a motor, but it does produce enough to cause the earphone to produce a sound. The earphone is a device that converts electricity into sound. If you connect the earphone to a regular battery, it will produce a loud cracking sound, **but do not put the earphone in your ear.** Hold it away from your ear because the sound is much louder than that produced with your weak "lemon, steel, and copper battery." Also, you may damage the earphone if you use too large a battery.

Lead acid batteries used in cars should not be used in your experiments because they produce a large flow of electrons. Car batteries contain lead, lead salts, and sulfuric acid, and use flat plates to produce large currents of electricity. This type of battery can be recharged and used over and over again to start a car. Scientists and engineers are working on new types of batteries that can be used in electric cars. In electric cars, the battery is used to run the engine—no gasoline is burned. These cars produce less pollution and may become common in the future.

You can try repeating this experiment with two identical nails or two new, shiny pennies. You should find that there is no sound because there can be no flow of electrons produced if the metals are identical. However, there may be a slight sound if the surfaces are at all different. Can you try other coins such as a dime or nickel with a penny or nail and see how the sound in the earphone changes?

SOUND FROM A COAT HANGER

MATERIALS NEEDED

Bare copper wire, 39 in. (1 m) long

Metal coat hanger

Wooden chair

Is a sound that comes through the air the same as a sound that comes through a metal? You will find out in this experiment. You will compare the sound of a vibrating coat hanger as the sound travels to your ears through the air and through a metal wire.

Twist the middle of a bare, uninsulated copper wire around the hook of a metal coat hanger three times. If you hold the ends of the wire, the coat hanger should hang in the air, suspended from the wire. Now swing the coat hanger enough to knock it against a chair, as shown in Figure A. Repeat this several times and listen to the sound the hanger makes. After the hanger strikes the wooden chair, can you see the hanger vibrate or move rapidly back and forth?

Wrap one end of the wire one time around your right index finger and push your right thumb against your index finger to hold the wire in place. Wrap the other end of the wire one time around your left index finger and push your left thumb against your index finger to hold the wire in place. Press the tip of your right index finger against your right ear. Press the tip of your left index finger against your left ear. Now move your head enough to swing the

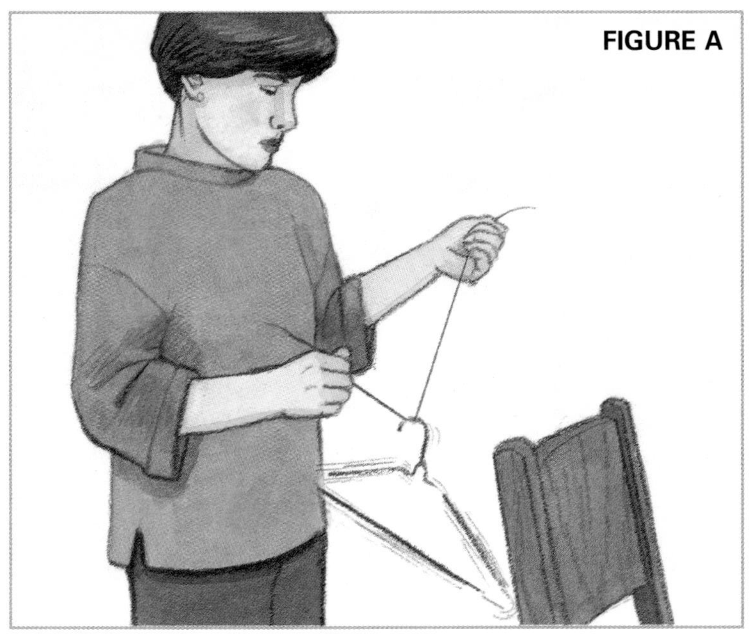

coat hanger and knock it against a wooden chair, as shown in Figure B. Repeat this several times and listen to the sound that comes through the metal to your ears. What do you hear?

Our brains interpret vibrations that reach our ears as sound. The vibrations that cause sound can travel through a gas, liquid, or solid, but they cannot travel through a vacuum, such as outer space.

When the coat hanger used in this experiment strikes the chair, it begins to vibrate. You may be able to see some of these vibrations as the hanger moves back and forth. You probably found that the sound of the hanger was quite different when it came to your ears through the metal wire instead of through the air. The sound through the wire is much louder and has a deeper, more resonant quality, like the sound of a heavy bell ringing. Coming through the air, the sound is faint and tinny. Also, the sound coming through the wire lasts longer than the sound coming through the air.

The vibration of an object causes the gas, liquid, or solid it touches (the medium) to compress and expand rapidly. As the object moves outward, it causes the medium to compress. As the object moves inward, it causes the medium to expand. This alternating compression and expansion causes sound waves to travel through the medium, like ripples spread across a pond in which a stone is dropped.

Sound waves can be described by frequency, intensity, and quality. Frequency is the number of vibrations per second, called *hertz*. Humans can hear sound waves that vibrate in the range of 20 to 20,000 hertz. Intensity is determined by the amplitude, or strength, of the sound waves. The strength of the sound waves depends on the energy put into making the sound. Quality depends on the number of different vibrations that may be present and how they combine. The sound may be pleasant, like music with many regular vibrations, or the sound may be unpleasant, such as noise with a number of irregular vibrations.

The speed of sound in the air is about 1,132 ft per sec (345 m per sec), but the speed of sound in copper is 11,680 ft per sec (3,560 m per sec). We see that the speed of sound is about 10 times faster in copper than it is in air. The speed of sound in steel is about 15 times faster than in air.

Sound travels slower through air than through metal because the molecules in air can be compressed, or pushed together, more than the atoms in a metal. The more a medium can be compressed, the slower the speed of sound through that medium. Since sound travels more efficiently through a metal, the sound you hear through the wire is louder and has a different quality than the sound you hear through the air.

Geoscientists use sound in solids to explore for underground oil. A small explosion, on the surface or underground, is used to generate a burst of sound waves. As these sound waves travel through the ground, they bounce off layers of rock. Sound travels slower through liquids than through solids. By timing how long it takes the sound waves to return to the surface, scientists can determine whether oil may be present and how deep it may be under the ground.

12

SOUND FROM CRUSHING METAL

MATERIALS NEEDED

- Two empty aluminum beverage cans
- Aluminum can crusher (optional)

Many metals make a sound when they are bent or crushed. Did you know this sound is caused by groups of metal atoms moving over one another? To learn more, try this experiment.

Place an empty aluminum beverage can in a can crusher and carefully listen as you crush the can. Repeat the experiment with another empty aluminum beverage can, but this time crush the can more slowly. If you do not have a can crusher, you can still get a sound from an empty aluminum beverage can by squeezing its sides.

The atoms in metals are packed closely together in a regular, repeating pattern called a metal crystal. The atoms in metal crystals can move over one another when a force is applied to the metal, as in hammering a metal into a sheet.

In many metals, a sound is made when atoms in the metal crystals move over one another. As you crush the empty aluminum beverage can, the sound you hear is caused by aluminum atoms moving over one another.

Tin is a metal often referred to as a "crying metal." Some people think tin sounds like someone crying as it bends.

13

TURNING A NAIL INTO AN ELECTROMAGNET

MATERIALS NEEDED

- Insulated wire, about 15 ft (450 cm) long
- Large steel nail, about 3 in. (7.5 cm) long
- 6-volt lantern battery
- Box of small steel nails
- Piece of paper

Have you ever seen a picture of a crane with an electromagnet lifting scrap iron or old cars? In this activity you will make a small electromagnet and learn how an electric current can generate a magnetic field in steel or iron.

Leaving about 12 in. (30 cm) of extra wire, begin wrapping the rest of the insulated wire in a tight coil around a large nail, as shown in Figure A. Begin at the head of the nail and wrap the wire toward the point of the nail. When the wire wrapping is almost 0.5 in. (about 1 cm) from the point of the nail, start wrapping the wire back toward the head of the nail. Continue this process until you have wrapped the wire about 150 times around the nail. Leave at least the last 12 in. (30 cm) of the wire free. Remove about 0.5 in. (about 1 cm) of insulation from each end of the wire.

Connect one end of the wire to the positive terminal on the battery. Place about 20 small steel nails on a piece of paper, and place the point of the large, wire-wrapped nail on top of these nails. Now touch the other end of the wire to the negative termi-

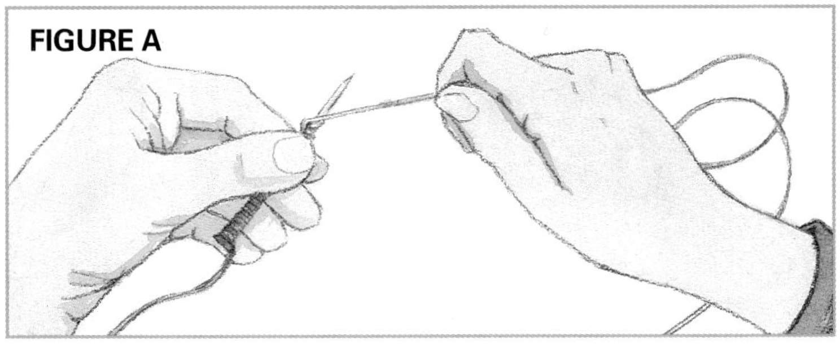

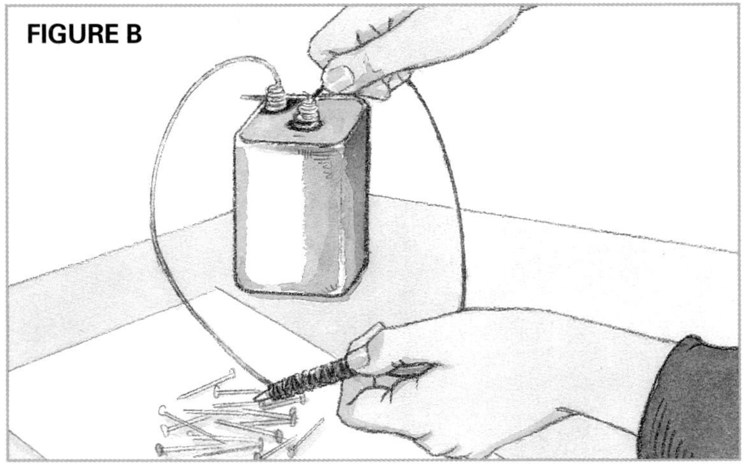

nal of the battery, as shown in Figure B. Lift the large nail above the paper. What happens to the small nails?

While holding the large nail in the air, remove the wire from the negative terminal of the battery. What happens to the small nails? Do they all fall off? Do some small nails cling to the larger nail longer than others before they fall?

Before connecting the wire to the battery, you should observe that the small nails are not attracted to the large, wire-wrapped nail. However, after you complete the circuit by connecting both ends of the wire to the battery, many of the small nails should stick to the large, wire-wrapped nail. Several smaller nails may hang together because the magnetic field in one nail can produce a magnetic field in the next nail and so on. You should find that the magnetic field is strongest at the point of the large nail. Small nails will be most attracted to the point of the large nail.

When you complete the circuit by connecting both ends of the wire to the battery terminals, electrons flow through the wire. These moving electrons generate a magnetic field. This field is just like the field in a regular permanent magnet, except that the field only lasts as long as the current is flowing. When the circuit is broken by removing a wire from the battery, the electron flow stops and the magnetic field is turned off.

After the current was stopped, you probably found that some of the nails continued to cling to the steel nail, which is mostly iron. The current, passing through the coils of wire, magnetizes the steel nail. The steel nail in the center of the coils makes the magnetic field stronger and may retain some magnetism even after the field is turned off. This is why you see a few small nails continue to cling to the wire-wrapped nail. However, if you knock the small nails off, the magnetic field may be lost, and the wire-wrapped nail may not act as a magnet until the current flows through the wire again.

Iron and steel are *ferromagnetic* metals that have a strong attraction toward magnets. Ferromagnetic substances consist of a number of small domains, or regions, of magnetism. The iron atoms in these domains act like tiny magnets with north poles lined up in the same direction. An external magnetic field such as the one caused by the current passing through the wire causes all the magnetic domains in the iron to line up in the same direction. When many of the individual domains are oriented, or line up, in the same direction, the ferromagnetic substance becomes magnetic. This orientation may last even after the current is disconnected so that the nail remains somewhat magnetic and may hold on to a few of the nails.

Magnetic resonance imaging (MRI), which uses superconducting electromagnets, allows a doctor to see inside a person's body. When a person is placed inside a large, strong magnetic field, the tiny magnetic fields in hydrogen atoms found in the water molecules of the body line up with the external magnetic field. Radio waves change the orientation of the hydrogen atoms in the magnetic field and these changes are detected. Different body organs contain different amounts of water and react differently to the external magnetic field and radio waves. A computer receives information from the MRI system about these differences and constructs a picture of the inside of a person's body. Doctors use these images to look for cancer or detect other health problems.

EFFECTS OF A MAGNET

MATERIALS NEEDED

Compass
Two flat magnets
Pencil
Steel nail
Penny
Aluminum foil

Have you ever felt the pull of a magnet toward another magnet or a piece of iron? In this activity you will explore the effects of magnets on one another as well as on different metals.

Set a compass on a table with no magnets close to it. One end of the magnetic compass needle will point toward the north. This end of the compass needle is called the *north pole*. Bring your magnet toward the north side of the compass. Find one side of your magnet that will repel the north pole of the compass. When a north pole of a magnet is brought close, the compass needle will turn and face in the opposite direction. Use a pencil to mark an *N* on the side of the magnet that repels the compass needle. The *N* will mark the north pole of this magnet. Mark the opposite side of the magnet with an *S* for *south pole*.

Repeat the above procedure using the second magnet. Find the north pole of the second magnet and mark it with an *N* in the same way you did with the first magnet. Mark the opposite side of the magnet with an *S* for south pole.

Now that you have identified the poles of the magnets, you

will explore the effects of one magnet on another magnet. Bring the north pole of one magnet close to the north pole of the second magnet. What happens? Bring the south poles of each magnet close together. What happens? Finally, bring the south pole of one magnet close to the north pole of the other magnet. Do you feel a push or a pull as the magnets are brought close together?

Next, you will test the effect of one magnet on several different metals. Set a steel nail, a penny (newer pennies are zinc with a copper coating), and a small piece of aluminum foil on a flat surface. Touch a magnet to each piece of metal, raise the magnet, and see if any of the metals can be picked up with a magnet. Try both the north pole and south pole of a magnet. Does it make any difference which pole of the magnet is used? Are any of the metals attracted to the magnet?

You probably found that the north poles from two different magnets brought close together seemed to push each other away. This same repulsion occurs when two south poles are brought close together. However, when north and south magnetic poles are brought together, there is an attraction that pulls the magnets together. In other words, like poles repel and unlike poles attract, as shown in Figure A.

The compass used in this experiment has a magnetic needle that swings on a pivot and lines up with the earth's magnetic field in a north-south direction. The end of the compass needle, or any

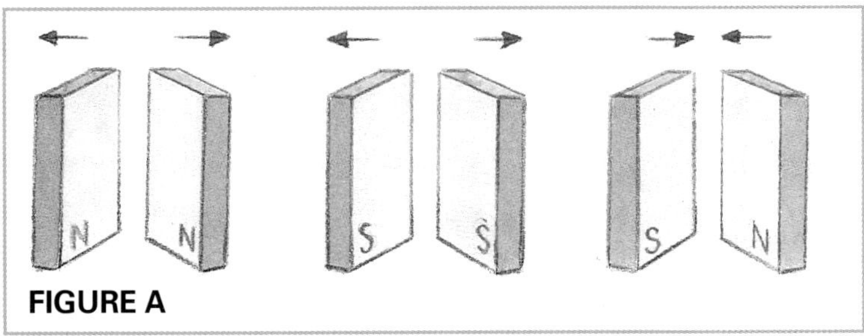

FIGURE A

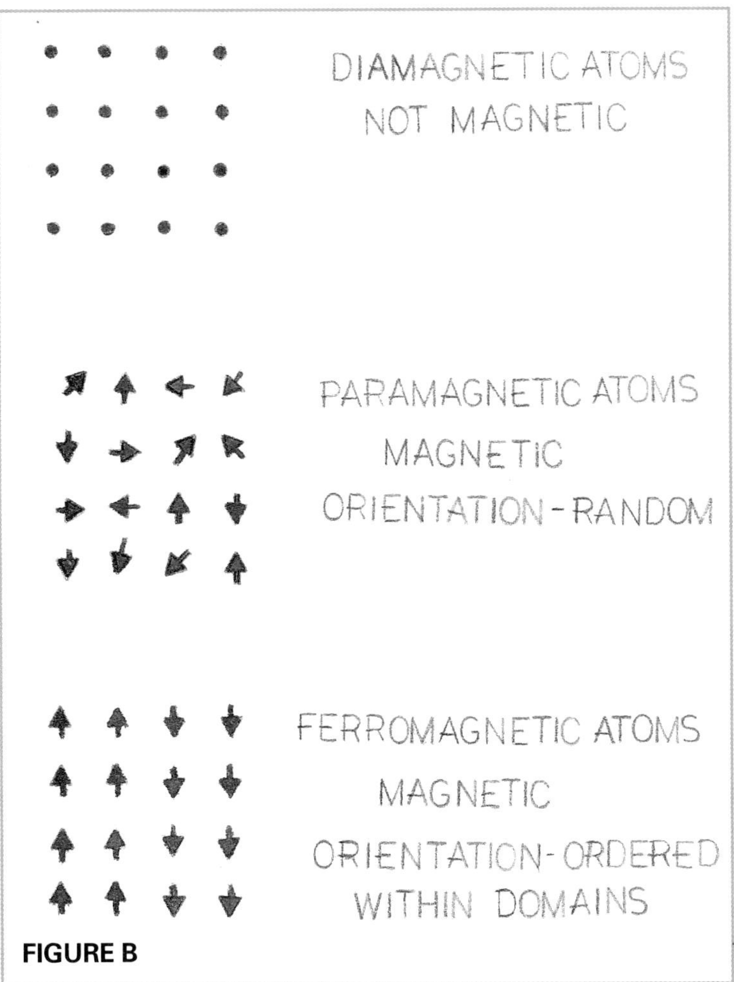

FIGURE B

other freely swinging magnet, that points toward the north is referred to as the north pole. The opposite end, which points toward the south, is called the south pole.

A magnet always has both a north and south pole. It is not possible to have a piece of magnetic material that has only a single pole—north or south. Magnets are made of individual atoms, each acting as a tiny magnet. Every atom has a north and south pole. If these atomic magnets are lined up facing the same direction, the whole material acts like a magnet with a north pole on one side and a south pole on the opposite side.

Not only can magnets attract or repel other magnets, they can also attract or repel other metals. In your experiment, did you observe that neither the aluminum foil nor the zinc and copper penny were attracted to your magnet? Was the steel nail—which is mostly iron—attracted to either the north or south pole of a magnet?

As shown in Figure B, there are three different kinds of interactions in the presence of a magnet, depending on whether a substance is *diamagnetic*, *paramagnetic*, or ferromagnetic. A diamagnetic substance, such as copper or zinc, obtains a magnetization that is opposite and repulsive to an external magnet. The individual atoms are not magnetic. A paramagnetic substance, such as aluminum, has atoms that act like tiny magnets, and these will tend to line up with and be attracted to an external magnetic field. However, both of these effects are quite small and can only be detected with special devices that measure the tiny effects of a magnetic field on the weight of an object.

Substances that are ferromagnetic, like iron, have regions within the solid where the magnets of the atoms are oriented in the same direction. These regions of common magnetic orientation are called *domains*. Because these domains can be lined up with an external magnetic field, a ferromagnetic substance is strongly attracted to a magnet. Did you find the steel nail was attracted to the magnet?

REFLECTING ENERGY

MATERIALS NEEDED

- Aluminum foil (preferably heavy-duty)
- Battery-powered portable radio
- Newspaper

Metals are good conductors of heat and electricity. Some metals are also good reflectors of radiant energy. In this experiment you will learn more about radiant energy and the reflection of radiant energy by metals.

For this experiment you will need a piece of aluminum foil that is about twice as large as the portable radio you are using. Also, this experiment works best with heavy-duty aluminum foil because it is thicker. If you do not have heavy-duty aluminum foil, you can double the thickness of regular aluminum foil by folding a piece in half.

Try to do this experiment as far away from large buildings as you can. Take the radio, aluminum foil, and newspaper outside. Turn on the radio and tune in a radio station. Hold the radio out in front of you with the speaker facing you. With your free hand, hold the sheet of aluminum foil just behind the radio, as shown in Figure A. While staying in the same spot, slowly turn completely around. As you turn around you should notice that the radio signal fades in and out, or that static appears and disappears.

If you have tuned in a particularly strong radio station, you may not notice any change in the radio signal as you turn around.

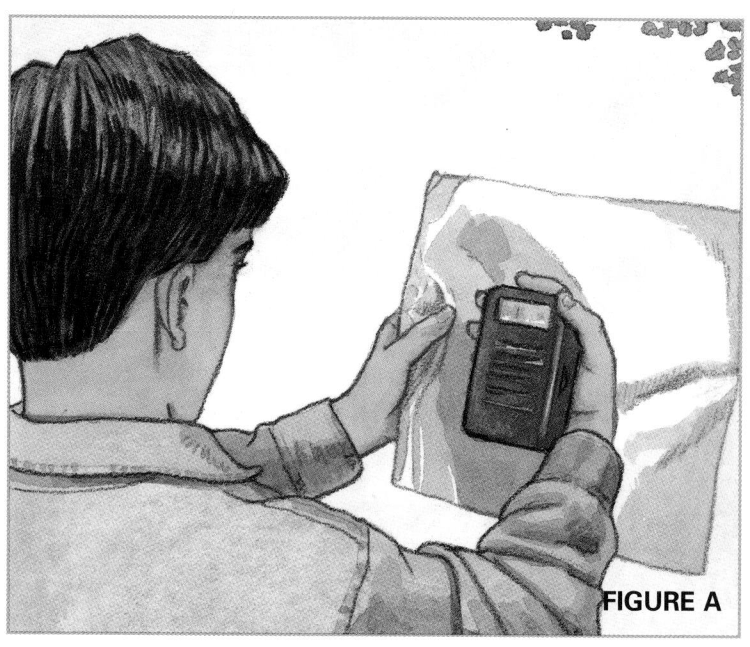
FIGURE A

If this is the case, tune in another station and repeat the experiment. Try both FM and AM stations. Does it matter if the radio signal is FM or AM?

Next, hold the newspaper behind the radio and turn completely around. Does the radio signal fade? Does the radio signal fade more with the newspaper or with the aluminum foil behind the radio?

Radio waves are a form of radiant energy. Radiant energy is energy that travels in a wave motion, similar to the moving ripples in a pond of water that are created after you throw in a rock. Some other forms of radiant energy include microwaves (used in microwave ovens for cooking), infrared radiation (the heating coils in electric toasters and stoves are sources of infrared radiation), visible light (the colors of the rainbow), ultraviolet, or UV, light (certain UV light causes light skin to tan), and X rays (used in medicine).

You cannot see radio waves, but they are all around you.

When you tune in a radio station, your radio receives the radio waves being transmitted by that station. Your radio changes the energy of these radio waves into sound waves, which come out of the radio's speaker.

The radio signal fades as you turn around while holding the aluminum foil next to the radio because the aluminum foil blocks the radio waves being transmitted to your radio. The aluminum foil blocks the transmitted radio waves by reflecting the radio waves away from your portable radio. As the radio waves hit the aluminum foil, they bounce off, like a ball bouncing off a wall or ripples bouncing off the sides of a tub of water. The position of your radio when the radio signal fades the most gives you a general idea of the direction of the radio station's transmission tower.

The radio signal does not fade when you turn while holding the newspaper next to the radio because the radio waves are not reflected away by the newspaper. Instead, the radio waves pass through the newspaper and are received by your radio, which changes them into sound.

Do you think wood or plastics reflect radio signals? How can you find out?

Aluminum is an excellent reflector of other forms of radiated energy besides radio waves. Some fire-fighting suits contain aluminum foil to reflect heat away from the person wearing the suit. Aluminum foil is also used as building insulation, and is used in cooking to keep heat either in or out of food.

Radar stands for "radio detecting and ranging." A radar system consists of two components, a transmitter and a receiver. Certain objects reflect radio waves. During operation, radio waves are sent out from a transmitter and travel through the air until they strike an object or target. A portion of the radio waves that strike the object is reflected by the object back to the radar system receiver. Since radio waves travel at a constant velocity, the delay between the transmission of the radio waves and the reception of the reflected radio waves gives the range of the object from the radar system.

How well an object reflects the radio waves of a radar system is called the *radar signature* of the object. A metal object generally has a large "radar signature" because metals reflect radiant energy like radio waves efficiently. Interestingly, even though the U.S. Stealth bomber (called the B-2) and the U.S. Stealth fighter (called the F-117A) are made of metal, they have extremely small radar signatures. They are coated with layers of special radar-absorbing material, and because of their unique shapes, they tend to scatter the radar signal so little of the signal returns to the radar receiver. Can you think of other useful ways that metals could be used to trap or reflect radiant energy?

16

METALLIC LUSTER

MATERIALS NEEDED

Two old pennies

Two old quarters

A mild metal polish (such as Twinkle)

Paper towels

Alert! Adult supervision needed. Before beginning the experiment, make sure to read and follow the directions on the label of the metal polish.

Why does a piece of metal shine brilliantly after being polished but over time become tarnished and dull? To find out, try this experiment.

Choose two pennies that are equally tarnished and two quarters that are also equally tarnished. Tarnished coins will appear dull and are usually old. Follow the directions on the label of the metal polish and polish one of the pennies and one of the quarters. Compare the polished coins to the tarnished coins. The polished penny and quarter should shine brilliantly while the tarnished coins still appear dull.

The brilliant shine seen on a polished metal surface is called *metallic luster.* Metallic luster is due to the special way visible light is reflected from a metal surface. The surface of a polished metal reflects nearly all the visible light that strikes the surface. Very little of the light is absorbed or taken in by the metal.

Visible light that appears white, like the light from the sun or from an incandescent lightbulb, is actually made of all the colors in the rainbow. Since most metals reflect all the colors in white light, they have a silvery white metallic color.

A few metals are colored because they do not reflect all the colors in white light. Gold, which appears yellow, and copper, which appears red-orange, are two examples of colored metals.

When metals become tarnished, their surfaces appear dull rather than lustrous or shiny. Tarnish is caused by dust and dirt or by metal atoms on the surface of the metal combining with chemical substances in the atmosphere. Usually, when metal atoms combine with other chemical substances, they can no longer reflect visible light efficiently. Instead, the combined metal atoms actually absorb some of the visible light. This is why tarnished metal usually appears dark in color in addition to appearing dull. Metal polishes remove tarnish by chemically changing the metal atoms on the surface of the metal that have combined with other substances back to a noncombined, or free, state.

Polished metals have been used for centuries to make mirrors. Flat household mirrors usually consist of a very thin film of silver or aluminum metal coated on one side of a sheet of glass.

Musical compact discs, or CDs, are based on the principle that metals reflect visible light efficiently. A CD has microscopic pits arranged in a spiral track approximately 3 mi (5 km) long. The microscopic pits are so small that a human hair can cover nearly 60 of the tracks. Encoded in these pits is the signal information for the CD player. The pits are etched in a thin layer of metal protected by an outer layer of transparent plastic.

A CD player uses a small laser to read the signal information encoded or stored in the microscopic pits. Visible light from the laser is reflected to a detector when the laser light beam passes over a flat part of the disc, but the light is not reflected to the detector when the beam passes over a microscopic pit. Since the disc is spinning rapidly, the detector sees the equivalent of light turning off and on very rapidly. This turning off and on of light is converted into an electrical signal, which is then sent to speakers, where it is changed into sound.

SCIENCE CONCEPTS

FURTHER READING

To explore further the properties of metal:

Darling, David. *From Glasses to Gases: The Science of Matter.* New York: Dillon Press, 1992.

Kerrod, Robin. *Material Resources.* New York: Thomson Learning, 1994.

Mebane, Robert C., and Thomas R. Rybolt. *Adventures with Atoms and Molecules: Chemistry Experiments for Young People.* 4 vols. Hillside, New Jersey: Enslow, 1985–1992.

Peacock, Graham, and Cally Chambers. *The Super Science Book of Materials.* New York: Thomson Learning, 1993.

VanCleave, Janice. *Janice VanCleave's Chemistry for Every Kid.* New York: Wiley, 1989.

Whyman, Kathryn. *Metals and Alloys.* New York: Franklin Watts, 1988.*

* *No longer in print, but you may be able to find a copy in your school or public library.*

INDEX